WORDS OF A TROUBLED SOUL

WORDS OF A TROUBLED SOUL

DAVID WILLIAMS

J. Merrill
PUBLISHING

J Merrill Publishing, Inc.
434 Hillpine Drive
Columbus, OH 43207
www.JMerrill.pub

Library of Congress Control Number: 2022918141
ISBN-13: 978-1-954414-56-3 (Paperback)
ISBN-13: 978-1-954414-55-6 (eBook)

Book Title: Words of A Troubled Soul
Author: David Williams
Cover Artwork: Kari Fagan-Mizer

For my Family

INTRODUCTION

Words of A Troubled Soul is inspired by and a modern twist to the "Chicken Soup for the soul" series. Everyone has been through something in their lives and sometimes the best way to let it out isn't violence as it's though creative writing. So here is " Words of A Troubled Soul" the intro, after this the next book will be announced in the near future inviting any and everyone who'd like to share their poems, short stories or any writings they choose. If you don't write and you've been through something I encourage you to write it down share your story you never know what words might help the next person. That is what this series is about sharing and inspiring, motivating and uplifting one another because we all go through our own struggles and we all need an outlet.

1

SOBRIETY

The moderator crossed his legs and straightened his dark-rimmed glasses. A hush fell over the group gathered in the church basement as each of the men seated knew the meeting was about to begin in earnest.

"Thank you all for coming out tonight. We have a new member with us tonight." He looked directly at me. "As is our tradition here, why don't you go ahead and introduce yourself."

He waved a hand in my direction as I shifted in my seat. I stood up on shaky legs and cleared my throat, shuffling my feet once I felt my legs stabilize.

"Hello. My name is...." I paused, looking at the floor. "You know what? That's not important right now."

I pulled my head up and looked each man in the eye.

"What you want to hear is my story. You want me to pour out my heart and commiserate in my sorrow, then somehow find a reason to celebrate my sobriety, right?"

My comment struck the proper chord as each man's expression confirmed I was right. "As long as I can remember, I've been battling this addiction. God knows how long it's been. I stopped counting the years. At first, I didn't want others to know I did it as an escape and felt weak inside. The reality is drinking made me numb. My failures and disappointments didn't feel as harsh when I was drunk. They disappeared.

"I forgot the pain I caused other people. It allowed me to escape the suffering I felt at the thought of someone else being in agony over what I'd done. Hell, it allowed me to forget the pain I inflicted on myself. And I liked it."

At this, the other men nervously shifted in their seats, half acknowledging a truth none dared admit.

"If you want to know what I drank, it was whatever someone poured into my cup. It didn't matter what it was; I drank it all. If you're wondering how much I drank in a day, that's simple. For breakfast, I started with four quick Icehouse Edges to get going. It was a fifth of Irish whiskey, four beers, and a shot of Bourbon for lunch. At dinner time, I finished off the Bourbon, drank another four beers, and it was time to open a new bottle of Irish whiskey by then.

"At this point, I couldn't tell you how much I consumed. What I said was just a rough guess of what I did. It could've been more. It could've been less; I don't know. That's how bad my addiction was.

Now, I manage to wake up every day and make it to work on time. But that only offered a distraction to what I really felt.

"Every day, the same pain, frustration, and agony in my soul would ravage my mind. I couldn't escape that pain, no matter what I did. The more I drank, the less I heard those voices whispering, 'you're not good enough.' It was a constant reminder that I had let my life slip away. And at my age, I don't have a lot of time left.

"I can't tell you how many nights I'd sit at my kitchen table staring at a bottle of Jack Daniel's and conversing with it. As if the answers to my life's problems could be found at the bottom of that bottle. I expected every bottle of whiskey to make me feel like I was home or as if my wife was hugging me again. But that's another story."

I cleared my throat and wiped a tear forming in my eye. I inhaled and exhaled deeply before continuing.

"The more I fell into the pit of alcohol, the more I thought about death. It crossed my mind so often that I wished I could drink enough to feel that cold embrace of death. Can you imagine? Rather than choose to live, I was hoping to die.

"Now, you can talk about your cold, clammy hands, how your body shakes when you don't drink. I've been there, too. But if I really ask myself, "how did I end up like this," I don't want to answer that question. I run away from the answer because the finger points at me, not you. And it's easier to blame this addiction on someone else.

"If I could say just a few more things. I never stood up for myself. I never spoke out against the things I knew were wrong. You couldn't find me marching in the streets to protest anything. I didn't care what was happening around me. Guess you could say I was selfish cause I never found a reason to speak up.

"Well, today, I need to speak up. I'm tired. I'm tired of wasting money on whiskey and pills to try and ease my depression. I'm tired of feeling, you know.

"I've been around long enough to know; you only get one chance at this life. There are no do-overs. You either live with purpose, or your soul dies every day. At this point in my life, after all, I've done, I gotta say. All I'm living for is knowing that this life will end soon."

"SHARING A STORY CAN INSPIRE, MOTIVATE, AND IMPACT THE NEXT."

2

POSSIBLE

Is it possible to kill yourself to escape the pain? Will God ever talk to me again? Hello, father, forgive me, but the wound was fresh on my flesh, feeling like it was growing, open for view to the people that had seen it grow without even knowing.

Is it possible for the pain to be like a scab on you hard in pain, and when it finally heals, the scar it leaves behind is the memory of that time the pain was present, and the hurt was real?

Is it possible to do wrong and change, but the past won't let it go, so you can't grow? It's hard for the new you to show.

Is it possible to still make it knowing you didn't protect your temple following the rules? It's not that simple, feelings you wish could change, but the feeling remains. Then you pray, and you walk into your season hold on...

3

BETTER PLACE

Hello? Momma? Papa?

Where are you?

It's so bright here.

As I walk, the ground looks gold.

I see grass still, but it's really low, and it's very soft.

As I walk back to the golden roads, I hear voices. As I walk closer, I see big houses (wow) that have names on them... wait, there is my name. I run to The big house. I open the door; it's amazing, mom! As I walk further into the house, I notice something that looks like a glass ball. I see you. Why are you crying, momma? Where are you? Where am I? The longer I look at you, the more I understand that I will not see you for a long time... I hear my name being called; I have to go. I'll come back to check on you, momma. I hope you know I'm okay and can't wait to see you again.

4

DARKNESS

Have you ever lived life and just wanted to give up, not realizing that you are worth more to someone than you feel? Knowing what's gone hurts, and the thoughts only make it worse.

Praying for brighter days, but the thought of life is what hurts. Staying in the dark is easy because that's how your eyes see reality. The light is blinding something you can't see nor want to believe. Perception over reality, yet this is what your reality Perceives. Darkness surrounding lost hope, unable to see the light nor life worth living...

5

CAUTION

My heart it's been damaged

Love don't live here. It's on another planet.

Dreams are like stars; they exist but are too far to reach. Wanting to feel but have yet to heal, can I love love? I hurt from love. I can't deal with love, but love is on my mind. I would say heart, but that takes us back to the start, and love showed me that's not what love is. A kiss and an I love you turns for the worse, and realizing that that isn't love is what truly hurts. I want love; I need love. I thought I felt love, but now your love, and I think I love or even in love, so if you want to love, please proceed with caution... my love.

6

FATHER, CAN YOU HEAR ME

So many questions, and too impatient for the answers. So, I'll continue to live, laugh, and love. Trying to wait until I hear from you; the silence is suspenseful. Am I asking the right questions? Is it okay to ask without questioning you? You gave me two ears. I'm listening, Lord, I don't always listen, and that's my problem, but I'm trying harder. I have faith, yet I lack the vision. I feel like I'm talking to myself. I often pray for health or wealth. Times get rough, and that's just the cards that were dealt. I won't complain. Just curious if I'm wasting my time only because I'm in this conversation alone. I don't mean to be rude for asking, but father, can you hear me?

"ASKING FOR HELP SHOWS THAT YOU'RE READY TO HANDLE MORE, NOT THAT YOU'RE WEAK."

LOVES TIME LOOP, PT 1

Michael and his girlfriend, Sarah, had been together for three years. The love they shared knew no beginning or end. The limitless nature of this unshakable emotion naturally led to discussions of finally getting married and starting a family.

Coming from a large family, Michael wanted to enjoy that feeling by starting his own family. It was a point of contention between him and Sarah, as she was frightened by the idea of raising children. Abandoned at the age of three at a daycare center, she was told the Police were called by the director after her parents failed to pick her up for three consecutive days.

Her father, Richard, died in prison, and her mother, Denise, succumbed to alcoholism, feeling overwhelmed by her circumstances. Not learning proper coping mechanisms, she found alcohol would numb the pain in her life, telling herself she could control this habit. It was too late before Denise learned this was a grave mistake.

Sarah clarifies to Michael that they would be financially prepared to start a family when his designs for a new city-requested mall are approved. By then, she anticipated having a third restaurant location open and would be able to devote her attention to their family. She never speaks of the sheer terror she holds about starting a family. She's willing to try and overcome her worst fear.

Two weeks later, Michael is walking on the now barren ground where the mall will be built. Alone, he smiles, praying to God he finds the opportune moment to ask Sarah to be his wife. For months, he's wanted to ask her to join him in this next step of life, but his fears have gotten in the way.

Feeling he would be inadequate as a husband and father is only part of his reluctance to push forward.

His father's chronic drug use led him to abuse his mother. This remained hidden from Michael's knowledge until the age of seven. He watched in horror as his father held a knife to his mother's neck, threatening to kill her if she didn't give him her debit card. And then, his terror was elevated to unknown heights when he watched the police shoot and kill his father, ending the threat of his mother being killed.

Though he determined never to harm a woman long ago, that image of his father was permanently seared in his memory, causing him to wonder if he could overcome the fear of being a good man.

Realizing the sun is setting, he walks to his car and gets in. The engine on and the vehicle engaged in gear, he turns for home along the same route he's taken for years. Only this day, something would change the course of his life forever.

Michael never saw the semi-truck to his left. Striking the driver's side of the car, Michael's car flips over more than five times, coming to rest in the median. The truck ends on its side, landing with a thunderous sound against the pavement.

Within minutes, emergency personnel were on the scene, doing their best to rescue and save both drivers. The truck driver is lying on the ground several hundred yards from the crash. He wasn't wearing a seatbelt and was thrown from his vehicle. He's pronounced dead at the scene. To save Michael, the firefighters used the jaws of life to cut him out of his car. He's also unresponsive, and his pulse is weak, but he's alive.

Upon hearing the news of Michael's accident, Sarah rushes to the hospital, unconcerned with anything other than seeing him. Her heart whispers that part of her life has ended because her future husband and partner lie near death. Tears mingle with prayers as she speeds her way onward.

Days turn into weeks, then months and Sarah waits at Michael's bedside every day, praying he wakes up from the coma he's been in for what she believes is too long. Her family and friends do their best to help her cope with the pain, and she is grateful for the support she has in her life. But something in the back of her mind whispers that alcohol might help ease the pain as well... Suddenly, Michael wakes up to the sound of his brothers and sisters crying. He hears shouting outside the bedroom door, then a gunshot—his mother screams in terror, followed by another gunshot, then another. The wailing inside the bedroom grows louder while the voices outside have gone nearly silent. A knock on the door is followed by a uniformed officer stepping inside to inform them their father is dead.

Looking around, Michael realizes he is seven years old. Everything he had in life – his business deals, his career, his future, but most importantly, Sarah – has been taken from him. Once again, he is placed in the confines of his life's single most despicable moment.

Confused and enraged, he begins to weep, the tears stinging his cheeks. How did this happen? And how would he return to the life he was living only a few days ago?

To be continued...

8

NEXT LIFETIME

The pain was bottled up inside.
Laughing on the outside, yet on the inside, you cry.
Throwing your hands up because God knows you tried.
Every time I said I loved you and I heard it back, you lied.
Leaving me alone trying to figure out why.

Coming up with something to change,
and since it's change, you say I'll give it a try
The difference is in the words, but the same rules apply
Now you heard the truth yet believe a lie.
Many would look up and ask God why.

But I never talked to him beforehand.
Praying that the person would open up the door and change your life.
Keep finding lust, looking for a husband or wife.
Yet, in all the wrong places
Looking for love as if you've misplaced it.

Not understanding how love could bring you to this point
So you're here with a gun and a knife

thinking about how one pull or one swipe
would potentially put you in another lifetime,
and maybe you'll find love there.

Anger took over, and it's sad because what was supposed to be love
led to this, and this can't be what love feels like; I guess I'll never
know, maybe next lifetime.

9

ALONE

In a room surrounded by hundreds of people, Yet I'm still alone
Thousands of followers on every platform, Yet I stand alone

To hear the words "we love you," Yet I feel alone
I speak, they listen, I post, they mention, Yet I am alone

It takes being by yourself to understand self,
So when you're around love, you don't Feel so alone

10

CONGREGATION

God says to come as you are (don't take it to the extreme), but still do your best. It's just sad that he says that, then the people in the church look at you as crazy for coming at all... my God and your church are not the same. If he came back today, many people would still be in their Sunday's best in their Sunday seats. God knows, but they'll never meet. The doors of the church are open. Some of you Jesus wouldn't want to greet because you've pushed his children away trying to seek him, but you threw shade. You see who cast the first stone. I'm grown and want to rebel, knowing I need Jesus, but the church members pushed me to hell's doorstep now that the ship has sailed... in your eyes, but my God knew my heart.

"WHY WONDER WHEN YOU CAN KNOW."

11

FALLING

I got this so-called game of life in control, unlocking the cheat codes to make life's lessons unfold and attacking life head first, asking the universe what's worse. The good dying young or having two ears, able to hear someone's good advice warning them to avoid a situation they've made it out of, and it's not hitting either ear. We live in a *now* generation when *now* is past tense and *right now* is present.

Thinking what's best for me isn't trying to combine pain and love in the same person wondering why love is hurting. If you drop the ball, pick it up because it's your move when the ball is in your court.

12

MENTALLY GONE

AR-15 carried by someone 18 in a place where future teens learn, play, and sing. In a place where bells ring .....wait, the door to a class opens, and a disturbed teen enters, and instead of the class bells, shots ring, and the future of these children is ended. No longer able to become teens because an angry and bothered teen could have chosen the path of a scholar or been an athlete, cop, or barber. Instead, they took the lives of someone's son and daughter, to think life could have taken him so much farther if he had just... let... go. Pain bottled up inside allowed the anger to arise, and to everyone's surprise, he pulled the trigger, repeatedly neglecting the fact that what was done to him, he's doing to others.

Younger than him, they didn't even get a chance, but he did, and he chose to murder wives, mothers, and kids, he had a chance to take what was done to him and become better, but this is what you get when frustration is confused...

13

POWER

Never feeling respected
Overlooked always neglected
pain is all you know
as you grow
tears turn to anger
as the abused gets old

Lashing out can be drastic.
In pain with a gun can be tragic
Mentally the triggers already pulled
Since you put your mind to it, you just do it

Not quit respect when fears in the heart
No longer overlooked
because the holder of the gun is in charge.
The abused start to abuse
and the cycle is a ride on another power trip.

"IF WE PRETEND TO BE SOMEONE
WE'RE NOT, THE WORLD MISSES
OUT ON THE REAL YOU."

14

FIREWORKS

As the people gather to watch the show, Eardrums ringing turn to booms as the colors light up the sky and shower down. Ever wonder why they are so loud, like gunshots? (BOOM) Then comes the pow; people jump in fear and say "wow" as their eyes light up. The one pow was the sound of the gun hidden by the fireworks. On this Fourth of July show, no one knows that something tragic happened because the BOOM turned to POWs, and the crowd goes WOW. Nobody ever noticed what was happening around them. One looks around, finally seeing that a mother's baby is bleeding out, and who's to blame? Could letting off shots to bring in the New Year be the cause? Maybe his purpose on earth was complete. "We want more!" As the crowd cheers and claps, his lung collapse, and just like that, it seems he's gone. Where'd the shots come from?

No one notices because all attention is in the sky, and timed perfectly, gunshots sound like an addition to the show. One in the lung. This world is insane. More people notice that someone has been shot; all attention is on him. Regret fills a few faces as they wish they would have noticed sooner. The friends that came with the individual surround him yelling and screaming. On the other side of the city, he had a praying grandmother. Every Fourth of July, she prays her family has a good time and makes it home because she sees the world getting worst. As he arrives at the hospital, the paramedics inform them of the young man they are bringing in. The one nurse recognizes him because she delivered his first child weeks ago. He is 25 years old and has been shot in the chest. It seems the bullet has exited his body, and he is unresponsive. Media moves fast. It hits the news no names have been released yet or suspects at the time. As his status is unknown, grandma watches and fears for her family's safety. Something in her spirit isn't right, so she prays and prays.

As grandma prays, she gets a knock at the door. It's her daughter. She says, "mom, I need you. They shot my baby boy, and I can't do this alone." Already dressed, grandma walks to the car singing, "Nothing but the blood of Jesus, Lord, I know you're able." They arrive at the hospital, and as the mother and grandmother enter, the doctors say they've got a pulse. As the two friends sit in the lobby in tears, a few moments later, the doctor comes out and says, "I'm not sure where you stand with religion," but something or someone had to have been looking out for me. As everyone in the lobby cries out, the grandmother smiles.

15

SOCIAL MEDIA

Never been able to fit in, wanting so badly to be accepted.
A quick glance as you scroll, you see but still, miss the message.
Reality is virtual because that's where you're invested;
if you're paying for likes, does that keep your pride protected?
Fear of no interaction has you remembering moments of feeling
neglected,
spending money to look the part and still getting rejected.

Being social is not the problem,
just don't get lost worrying about people
that wouldn't invest their time in you.

16

TEMPORARY

Pain is only a temporary inconvenience of the mind....

But temporary requires the acknowledgment
or measurement of time.
Is it possible to undo what the clock can't rewind?
No, no, no plays in my mind.

Putting on a smile doesn't make you fine
And laughter can't replace crying
But denying the fact that the pain is real is a sign....

The Bible says blessed are those who mourn....
So we weep;
something knowingly temporary brings great grief

So all we can do is pray
And believe that this pain is only temporary.

"IT'S OKAY TO CRY AS LONG AS YOU KNOW IT WILL NOT MAKE YOU CRY AGAIN."

17

LIFE

We live our days till we get old
Waiting for life's purpose to unfold
We make our rules and neglect what's told
Whatever it takes to reach the top
Taking down whoever tries to stop you
Wanting to believe that God's got you
You still take things into your own hands
Now, determine if this is God's purpose or your plan.

18

PRIDE

Push it to the side and tell me what you see, not what you think you see but what you know when you look. Seeing is believing, yet do you believe what you see? Don't let it cloud your judgment! If you could only see it, you'd know that it comes between many things, including family. Being the bigger person is hard when you're right and seems impossible when you're wrong. Don't let this get in the way; I've seen love get put on hold because of it, and relationships remain broken even with the tools to fix them all because you couldn't push it to the side. Pride has blocked a lot of blessings. The best thing to do is identify and control it before pride costs you everything.

"WHEN LOOKING FOR SUPPORT,
FURTHER FROM HOME TENDS TO
WORK BETTER."

19

PRESS PLAY

If you're hearing this recording, I've found out what happens after life. It's crazy because as I sit here thinking about my life, I realize with all the ambitious thoughts, I amounted to nothing.

Understanding that life isn't fair and harnessing negative energy towards the subject won't do anything but turn you into a negative person. Many would say you have a family that loves you and a great job as a manager, so you have something and someone(s) to live for. They're right, I do, and sometimes the best thing to do when you feel you can't get anything right is to look at all your mistakes and past failures. You think you're not what's best for the ones you love... even if you're no longer around, at least they can live without blaming you for messing up or falling short.

So I was driving one day and what was supposed to be a family trip took a turn for the worst; those voices came back once the children started arguing, and my wife started an argument about something we both barely knew. The voices in my head yelled shut up, shut up!!! As the words of my children and wife faded, turning into just loud noise that seemed to grow louder and louder. Shut them up, shut them up, the voices screamed. So I pulled out the handgun I had in my driver-side door slot, took the safety off, and with the voices in my head. My children were still arguing in the back seat, and my wife was arguing; the only thing I got from her was she was right as she called me stupid and inconsiderate. While she's not even looking at me, she's staring out the window, and I pull the trigger........

The morning comes, and the alarm clock goes off as it's time for work. That's all life has become, fulfilling someone else's dreams while I die in mine. That was the seventh time I've been killed in my dream this week, all from unspoken issues that have occurred over and over again, and since I haven't changed anything, I've gone insane, not killing others but erasing my name. After dying so many times, I've finally realized that the problems I have can't be solved if I'm dead, so I have to keep my head and play this recording when I'm close to the edge, and if you're listening to this, then that tells you something. If you ever need someone to listen, I have two ears. Not everyone has someone to speak to, and I get it. That's why I had to press record.

20

QUESTIONS

Trying to find the words to express my feelings, and even the dictionary couldn't define these thoughts of...(sigh) God, I hope it's not hereditary because when I'm good, I'm great. And when I'm bad, the thoughts are horrifying.

I want to feel complete, but as the saying goes, I'm looking at the glass half empty, trying to understand that this might not be the real me but the present me, so I'm left with this current reality. Why can't I choose not to have a choice? Will that be acceptable? What I am saying is something that's not even negotiable.

If I gave up free will, would you see that that was my choice but is that in your will? I can't give up free will because I would not be free to do your or my will, but isn't that the point?

Lord, forgive my question. I mean, questions. I want to be on point with your will. I want to be more, but ima afraid to fail, so I'll ask for your answer.

21

GOD'S TIMING

Today's the day! I got my clothes laid out, and my breakfast and lunch packed. Lord, I'm ready for this beautiful day you've woken me up for....

Not knowing that ahead of a sunny day was a dark clouded downpour. Skies were still clear as far as the eye could see, but the clouds were like the pain that came with the day just unseen.

"LIVE TO MOTIVATE CAN MOTIVATE
TO LIVE."

22

FAVOR

I've done wrong, I've done right, the wrong hurts and the right gets covered up, but I'll say I'm still here. Three attempts of suicide didn't work, people's words and actions towards me didn't work, and I'm still standing saying God Favors me. I've been judged and talked about, but God favors me. Many live better than me, but God favors me. I hate my life. I hate this world, but God favors me, so I'm gonna keep my head up and move on. Don't feel sorry for me. That's not the motive. Know that this is the season for "Favor."

23

LOOK UP

They say aim high, and you'll go far.

But what's that journey like to the stars you're aiming for? It's amazing how the highs will make you feel low.

Love will have you dancing with the devil like you sold your soul Perception of reality will have you lost in time.

Both hands are on your head like you have lost your mind. Often heard, do right, or you'll reap what you sow.

But it's too late. I messed up, and I'm trying to let it go. Funny how your dark past can haunt a bright future. Did no one see the change?

Or, like the news

I want to acknowledge the bad until it's well-branded. Then a voice said, "pick ya head up."

Your eyes are aimed down - impossible to aim high.

You've got to see it and believe it. So it starts with your eyes.

24

RESTING PLACE

Trying to find that peace of mind that leaves your mind at ease,
praying for that special place that brings your mind to peace.

Take me to that special place where faith will grow,
I've sinned in light and dark, and only God will know.

In that place, amazing grace, your voice will be that sweet sound.
I'll keep the faith you'll fill this place. That's how I'll know you're
around.

25

REFLECTION

This man has been through hell and back, as they say. Lost family, friends, and loved ones along the way, material items that held value in this world. I've witnessed him firsthand lose family members that raised him, yet he's kept a smile on in public, hiding the pain. When I see him, he cries, often punching things around him, causing physical damage, but that damage doesn't compare to the mental damage life has caused. Now I'm not justifying his destroying his home, but I understand.

This does not define him as a man because I've seen the best in him. He's gone above and beyond at anything he associates himself with. Have you ever felt like life gets harder with every move you make? I've seen the lost hope in his eyes. Knowing someone since kindergarten and staying friends through high school, all for someone to take his life before crossing the high school finish line. It's crazy because I've heard him talk about his friend all the time; when he makes bad choices or can't make up his mind, he would always say, "if he were here, he'd know what to do." I've watched him talk to himself, arguing about people he felt were his friends, not understanding that people are in his life for a reason or a season. I've been around yelling don't do it when he wanted to take his life. I've seen him at his best and his worst. I've seen him pray, and pray, and things get worse, and he still prayed, and one day, things got better for him. He met a woman to match his ambition, and they formed a family; continuing to pray, he saw some bad days and more good ones. As he lives, he notices there are more good days than bad, and he begins to thank God. Now when the man looks at himself, he no longer sees addiction, suicide, and hate; now, he sees hope and love and knows that life won't be easy, but through life and prayer, he found that God is able. Looking at this man, you would have never known his past. Looking at him now and the closer I look, I realize that the man is me, and I've learned that this world will have you unrecognizable to yourself, and God will turn your life around to the point where you can't believe it's you.

"WHEN YOU LOOK AT YOURSELF, SEE WHAT YOU DREAM OF BEING AND MAKE IT HAPPEN."

26

THANKFUL

Walking through a storm, yet this is not your typical storm.

I can feel the rain which symbolizes pain and represents the tears falling. Drops race down my face

Negativity surrounds me like a dark cloud. An umbrella couldn't stop this downpour.

Lightening, which symbolizes the reminder that the pain is present, comes every couple of minutes. A storm can last hours. So you try to weather the storm. Have you ever seen it rain for weeks?

That's how it feels when the rain doesn't seem to end, then you hear the boom and see lightning again. Feeling defeated knowing you can't win. So you pray for the storm to end and hear that prayer changes things. He's an on-time God, yet our times are not on the same clock, so it rains harder again. It's not physically raining, yet you feel like you're drowning, just painful enough to drive you insane. So you pray because you remember trouble don't last always and forever seems to have an end the more you pray, and when the devil says you lose, God says you win. As the sun starts to shine again, you realize that you're stronger than you thought, and you get to see the storm end.

27

COUSINS (F.O.E.)

G rowing up, I wasn't the thug; that was my cousin.

I tried to fit in, but it's like a thug in church or a pastor selling work, I wanted to fit in, but that didn't work. So I stuck to what I knew, the periodic table, and forming a hypothesis on why quicksand moves so slowly. Anytime it was time to head out, I got left behind, wondering if I ever crossed their mind when it was that time.

They say to get in where you fit in, so I managed the money and drugs as if it was a store and I was checking inventory. During the ride-outs, I was at the hideout counting money and doing homework, waiting on my day to make it out.

Seasons change, and it's time to graduate, years in the game, and nothing has changed. Except there are fewer of us, but that was out of my control. I could tell you profits and what was sold, but how the tragedies unfold that's a story untold. A day before walking across that stage left the barbershop; I got the dark fade.

Pulling off, a cop got behind me, cut his lights on, and sped right past me. I start to pull off after stopping for the police, and a car speeds past me. Another car comes flying by, and tinted windows turn to two guns pointed at me. Shots fly as they pull the trigger, and I feel two go right through me.

As I look down, I know I've been hit, thinking this is it. I looked over. They were getting out of the car. I tried to move, but the pain wouldn't let me get far. More gunshots, but these missed my car. I close my eyes and hear my cousin's voice telling me to hold on. Not able to feel anything, I ....

To be continued...

28

TIME

When you count the minutes, it only takes seconds; as you watch the minutes, it could take an hour. All you can do is add it up as the days change. Healing from pain can take days, weeks, or months. Counting to ten will calm you down. One, two, now it's been a year, and life has set in and a whole year wasted because you weren't you and wanted to fit in... don't waste life on past mistakes but planning to make your future great. Remember, it takes time.

29

FREEDOM

Free, at last, was never a thing of the past, just words often spoken that many looked passed; a purpose-driven life came to a crash when that purpose was introduced to hate from the past.

Free to walk around but mentally in cages overlooked and often neglected because it's been going on for ages, you can handle situations better? Here wear the skin I'm in.

Because the shoes may fit, you wear them but walk around the people you know in my skin; you might end up scaring them.

Free to play this game called life, whatever you land on is a possible outcome in life. Now spin. God's cheering for you and the devil sitting there with a grin, knowing the outcome even before you took that spin. Now once you see what you've won is when the game begins.

Free to live with the choice you've made, some good, some bad. People say it might send you to an early grave. At this point, pray and say, Lord, I love you. Protect me so that one day I might be truly free...

30

SELFISHLY SELFLESS

Pro-choice vs. pro-life... what about the choice to live? So many people say that abortions are bad, while many feel there are many good reasons to get on. Let's call those reasons the grey areas because rapes happen, and the woman getting pregnant should be able to make her choice.

On the other hand, you have a woman who's just promiscuous, and she gets pregnant by a guy she doesn't want to have a baby with. That's totally different from the first situation, don't you think?

Now they say it takes two... yet the man's decision is often ignored... now if the woman wants the baby and the man doesn't, and she has the baby, now is the father wrong for not being there if he let it be known from the beginning?

What if the man is excited to be a dad and can't wait, and the woman says, "Nah, I don't want it," and she aborts it? What about the man, then?

Now do me a favor; this may be difficult to do. Whatever side you're on, argue for the opposing side and see how that goes.

I only bring this up because I'm in the middle I see both views... I mean, this is the land of the almost free, isn't it?

31

WE THE PEOPLE

We can't breathe; no, you're not stopping my air flow by a knee.

But we can't breathe because we seek progression, and you won't let us succeed. Can we live?

From you, it's a no because my process to progression isn't yours, and even tho God opens up doors; you purposely closed yours.

We can't breathe!

Because family trees turn to a bush and slowly catch fire because envy engulfs desires, can we live?

Do right, drop the ball, and pick it back up.

Nope because the world laughs at you and says you've choked. It's funny how so many said You're asleep, yet your third eye stays awake. See, we uplift those around us while others will point and provoke.

So we can't breathe, not because someone is physically choking us but because the support is gone, the love is lost, and we're told to speak life, and the life is getting sucked out of us. They say the good life comes with a nice price, and I guess you're right. That's why Christ lost his... so why do we have to lose ours? No crime committed, yet, we're doing time, not behind bars, but these imaginary restraints are killing us.

It's time to change and break the chains that those have placed on us. Take the psychological knee off our brothers and sisters in Christ and hold on to what good we see in the world, even with a blindfold on, thanks to the media telling us what they want us to know. Enough is enough. Notice how we live to make something that says in God we trust, yet we remove the one nation under God and divide the "we." It's just y'all. Now you see why we can't breathe.

When you're so confused and torn between the two, understand they don't know the life and pain you've gone through. One side will say pray and believe. The other side says to believe what you see, not what you hear. One side will tell you about fear in Psalms 23, and the other will make you scared to believe. One side will say you can do all things through Christ who strengthens you; on the other, they'll make you feel weak. One side will say you belong in the kingdom, and the other will say you belong in the streets. One side will say you're enemies I'll beat, and on the other, they'll hate to admit defeat...

Conflicted.

32

SONGS OF JOY

As the man continued driving, he could feel his heart begin to harden, his insides churning as negative thoughts flooded his mind. He was in no mood to attend his weekly bible study tonight, but he would go, if only because he felt obligated.

He turns on the radio, and the first strains of a song he's heard a million times before begins lifting from the speakers. He turns the volume up, feeling his burden lighten a little. He starts to sing along with the song, turning the volume up as high as the radio would allow. By now, he was singing at the top of his lungs, crying as the joy from the song flooded his soul.

He realizes this is God talking to him now. There is no other joy he could feel without it being from God. It's more than amazing. As he continues singing and praising at full volume, the flash of red and blue lights catches his eye. Looking in the rear-view mirror, he is disappointed to see a police car behind him.

'Just my luck,' he thinks, pulling his car to the side of the road.

He turns the volume down a little, but the joy in his heart can't be stopped.

The officer walks to the driver's window, bending down slightly to peer into the car. "Sir, do you know why I've pulled you over?" he says.

"No, officer, I don't."

"I saw you swerving a little bit back there. Have you been drinking?"

"Uh, no, officer, I don't drink. It's just; this song came on and, I don't know, I just felt the Spirit do something in my heart, and I couldn't control it."

"Okay, can I see your license and registration, please?"

Handing the requested items to the officer, the man continues to praise the Lord in a much quieter tone.

"Sit tight." The officer returns to his cruiser.

After a few moments, the officer returns, handing the items back to the man. The man can tell the officer has been crying.

"I'll be honest," the officer says, "I've never heard of praising God as a reason for swerving in a vehicle, so this is a first. I don't know why you didn't just pull over as soon as you saw me, but I'm gonna' let you go with a warning. And, uh, next time the Spirit moves you, it's a good idea to pull over and let it happen like it just did for me."

The man smiled. "Thank you, officer. And God bless you."

"Thank you for this reminder. I apologize for interrupting. God bless you, too."

See – on the outside looking in, the man got a ticket for praising God. On the inside, looking out, the devil felt the man's spirit change the atmosphere in the car and wanted it to stop. He knows what you're going through and wants things to work in his favor.

If God inhabits the praises of his people, it's up to us never to allow the devil to have an opening to try and steal our joy.

33

COME ON BLACK MAN

Take pride in who you are, a proud man, and just because things didn't go as planned, you have to remember where you stand when the devil tries to rewrite your story, we must not forget God's plan, knowing we're in his hands. They said United, we stand, yet we remain divided and fall, separate, yet equal. Falling short of the standards that are not our own, reaching high yet touching low.

Come on, proud man, remember segregation isn't in the plan, not color nor race, sex nor gender, not gangs, no matter the street. To gain power, we must meet in the middle. Not coincidental, we are stronger than we expect, yet we forget that there are strengths in numbers.

Martin Luther king had a dream, and people don't want to see that dream. That dream may never come true. I say may because not all can see, but the few that can don't add up, and when the bad outweighs the fists lifted in support of the dream, it's only logical to lose hope in his plan.

Come on, black man, when we stood together, that was something they couldn't stand. So let's take ours.

"WHEN LIFE GIVES YOU PROBLEMS, MAKE SOLUTIONS."

34

MY GOD, MY GOD

My God is an awesome God. How about yours? My God created the heavens and the earth. He allows me to speak things into existence. I am glad my God is not like man; even when I'm wrong, he will not walk away and leave me. I love to praise him, "praise is what I do when I want to be close to him." I had trust in my God before reading Proverbs 3:5,6. After reading that, it just confirmed that if I trust in him and acknowledge him, he will direct my path. I should have been dead and gone so many times, but he kept me. My God is forgiving; my God is patient. He had made me qualified for jobs when I wasn't eligible to fill out the application. My God will do it. He has given me all the words to say when I've not known how to respond to a question or situation. If you don't believe me, try him out, don't pray and worry. Remember, faith without works is dead. So study to show thyself approved, and he will make a way for you. Keep on holding on; you don't need to be perfect. Look at my life.

Never forget God hears a sinner's prayer. That's why I say amen and walk into my season. Don't look back and remember the devil won't let this road smooth but know and believe that OUR God will see us through.

35

LET IT SHINE

Sweetheart, will you please stop singing? Your father is trying to give me the directions, so we don't get lost. (Singing fades) driving out of town as they always do every summer to get away. Around the bend, make a right, then hang left, and we have 68 miles, and we're there.

Does anyone want to play a game? Their daughter asked. Not right now, honey. Sit back and put your seatbelt on.

Slow down, her husband says as she passes a sign that says the speed limit, which his wife was going well over. The little girl begins to sing again after 45 minutes, "this little light of mine, I'm gonna let it shine," as she rolls her window down and sticks her hand out to feel the cool breeze on her fingertips.

The mother looks back and tells her daughter to bring her hand back in the window, taking her eyes off the road for a split second. Father looking down at the GPS, daughter rolls up the window. As the mother looks back at the road, she notices a deer running across. In an attempt to miss the deer, the mother swerves off the road. As the car goes off the road, the daughter screams, "Daddy," while the mother screams her husband's name, and the husband shouts, "JESUS," as the car flips and land upside down. The mother blacks out.

Everything is blurry. The mother looks around, picking herself off the ground, no longer in the car. She calls for her husband and daughter. As she stumbles back towards the car, still in her seatbelt, she sees her daughter sitting there, not moving.

The car explodes as the mother struggles to make it to her daughter. The mother falls to the ground crying, and after a few mins, she pulls herself together to try to find her husband. Judging by the windshield, he flew through it; the mother began to scream her husband's name. Then she sees him on the ground. As she crawls over to him, she hears her daughter's voice sing, "this little light of mine, I'm gonna let it shine." As she makes it to her husband, she realizes he has a tree branch that went completely through him.

After losing her daughter and husband, the mother falls to the ground, neglecting her injuries. She faints as she does she hears her husband's last words, and she cries out, "JESUS!"

"Everywhere I go, I'm gonna let it shine, let it shine, let it shine, let it shine. Jesus gave it to me...."

The mother's eyes open; she's in the hospital; she broke her neck and can't move it, but she sees the Doctor at the foot of the bed. The first thing he does is informs her about the injuries, yet all she can think of is her family. Crying because the last thing she remembered was she was the only one that made it.

The doctor says, "Ma'am, I'm not sure about your beliefs, but something or someone was looking out for y'all." The mother cries, saying, "I can't believe they're gone!"

The doctor says, "Ma'am, your daughter was in a burning car for God knows how long and only suffered several burns on the arms and legs. Your husband was thrown through a window, and a 4-inch tree branch went through him. We were able to remove it, and he should be out of surgery shortly. And for you, you broke your neck after being thrown from the car.

She hears, "all through this place, I'm gonna let it shine." As the mother looks to her side, she sees her daughter lying in a bed next to her, reaching her hand out for her mothers as they sing. Let it shine, let it shine, let it shine!

"DON'T BECOME COMPLACENT EVEN IF YOU'RE CONTENT."

36

WORK

When we are young, we are taught that we can be ANYTHING in the world as long as we work towards it. The older we get, the more we forget that the word "work" is what separates us. Some of us do, some don't, some of us will, and some won't. All you have to do is think it, believe it, and work towards what you want, and when you get there, you may be someone's motivation to work on themselves.

37

WILDEST DREAMS

The man's eyes were heavy as he forced them open. He blinks several times, focusing his attention on his surroundings. As his eyes take inventory of the room, he realizes this is still a dream, his subconscious somehow intruding upon his conscious thoughts.

He has no idea how he got here or when. All he knows is that he is confined by this space, unable to decipher why he is here or what purpose it may serve. Then, he slowly begins to look around the room and smiles.

Contained within these walls is everything he ever desired but did not have the means to acquire them. Filled with joy, his heart leaps at the thought of reaching out and touching all the things he dreamed about finally being in his possession.

This seemed a fitting reward in his present state of mind. Before this, the man attempted to take his own life. His failures weighed heavier on his mind than any accomplishment he achieved. But he has been spared, only to end up in this room, the pinnacle of his earthly desires.

Money is lying everywhere, more than he could count in his lifetime. There is every possible item his wife and children had wanted over the last three years suddenly come to life.

Or was it alive?

Filled with joy beyond comprehension, he dances, singing praises to the Lord and clapping his hands. Finally, he can provide for his family the way he always wanted to.

A cell phone ringing on a table pierces the silence. Curious, the man picks it up. "Hello?"

There is no answer. Shrugging, he hangs up the phone.

Situated next to the phone is a set of keys to the car of his dreams. Once more, the bliss of his soul exudes in shouting and praising Jesus for the blessings he is about to hold in his possession.

Once more, the phone rings. Jolted back to a form of reality, he picks up the phone. This time, there is a sinister voice speaking to him.

"Wrong person," the voice says.

Immediately, the person begins cackling, sending a shiver up the man's spine. This sound is hideous and evil in its volume. Thankfully, the call is disconnected. He places the phone on the table once more.

His eyes are suddenly drawn to a piece of paper he hadn't noticed until now. Squinting to read the print, he realizes this is a contract. He picks it up and carefully reads it.

'All of these things can be yours, and more. To gain possession of them forever, sign your name here.'

There is a blank space awaiting his signature below these words. Recoiling, he shakes his head.

"No. No, there is more than this," he says.

He drops the contract on the floor and begins walking toward the door out of the room. "What God has for me is for me," he says as he exits the room, never looking back.

Within moments, the items inside the room are consumed by fire, engulfing the entire room in a white-hot flame. The money; the car; everything he could ever want is suddenly rendered worthless, disappearing in a cloud of smoke and ash.

Don't let the devil fool you. God has greater things in store for you than you can imagine. Be blessed.

38

"TAKE WHAT MAKES YOU HAPPY AND LET THAT TAKE YOU WHERE YOU WANNA GO."

ABOUT THE AUTHOR

David A. Williams Jr. has always had a creative and entrepreneurial mind; growing up is what allowed him to become more attached to writing. His relationship with God shows in his work, not neglecting the fact that we are all human. In Words of a Troubled Soul, David mirrors his feelings and takes on life through his work.

This book starts like David's rough, dark, and hopeless life, and as you continue to read, you'll notice some helpful sayings and quotes along the way. As you reach the middle and end of the book, you'll see that his writings become brighter and display hope.

David wanted this series introduction to show that it's okay to think and feel how you do, and for him, he said in the light and the dark, he kept God in the midst. The last thing he mentioned was that there are so many troubled souls in this world, and he wants to put the brave ones in this series.

www.ingramcontent.com/pod-product-compliance
Lightning Source LLC
Chambersburg PA
CBHW031217120626
46545CB00003B/878